CHART HITS NOW!

LET IT GO

FROM THE HIT FILM 'FROZEN'
...PLUS 11 MORE TOP HITS

GW00507647

Published by
Wise Publications
14-15 Berners Street, London W1T 3LJ, UK.

Exclusive Distributors:

Music Sales Limited
Distribution Centre, Newmarket Road,
Bury St Edmunds, Suffolk IP33 3YB, UK.

Music Sales Pty Limited
Units 3-4, 17 Willfox Street,
Condell Park, NSW 2200, Australia.

Order No. AM1009327
ISBN: 978-1-78305-690-3
This book © Copyright 2014 Wise Publications,
a division of Music Sales Limited.

Unauthorised reproduction of any part of this
publication by any means including photocopying
is an infringement of copyright.

Edited by Jenni Norey.
Cover design by Tim Field.

Cover image Igor Zhuravlov/Fotolia.
Ricky Wilson photo by Anthony Harvey/Getty Images.
Christina Perri photo by Chelsea Lauren/Getty Images for Clear Channel.
Idina Menzel photo by Jamie McCarthy/Getty Images for Family Equality Council.
John Legend photo by Frazer Harrison/Getty Images.

Printed in the EU.

Piano • Vocal • Guitar

CHART HITS NOW!

LET IT GO

FROM THE HIT FILM 'FROZEN'
...PLUS 11 MORE TOP HITS

WISE PUBLICATIONS
part of The Music Sales Group
London / New York / Paris / Sydney / Copenhagen / Berlin / Madrid / Hong Kong / Tokyo

Your Guarantee of Quality:

As publishers, we strive to produce every book
to the highest commercial standards.

This book has been carefully designed to minimise awkward page turns
and to make playing from it a real pleasure.

Particular care has been given to specifying acid-free, neutral-sized paper
made from pulps which have not been elemental chlorine bleached.
This pulp is from farmed sustainable forests and was produced
with special regard for the environment.

Throughout, the printing and binding have been planned to ensure a sturdy,
attractive publication which should give years of enjoyment.

If your copy fails to meet our high standards, please inform us
and we will gladly replace it.

www.musicsales.com

ALL OF ME • JOHN LEGEND • 14

COMING HOME • KAISER CHIEFS • 20

HEART'S ON FIRE • PASSENGER • 7

HUMAN • CHRISTINA PERRI • 28

LET IT GO • IDINA MENZEL • 34

MAGIC • COLDPLAY • 42

NOBODY TO LOVE • SIGMA • 48

RATHER BE • CLEAN BANDIT FEAT. JESS GLYNNE • 52

ROYALS • LORDE • 58

SAY SOMETHING • A GREAT BIG WORLD
FEAT. CHRISTINA AGUILERA • 63

STAY WITH ME • SAM SMITH • 70

YOUNG BLOOD • SOPHIE ELLIS-BEXTOR • 74

Heart's On Fire

Words & Music by Michael Rosenberg

1. Well, I

© Copyright 2014 Sony/ATV Music Publishing.
All Rights Reserved. International Copyright Secured.

don't know how__ and I don't__ know why._____ But when

some-thing's liv-ing, well, you can't say die. You

feel like laugh-ing but you start to cry._____ I

don't know how__ and I don't__ know__ why._____

8

2. Well, I

don't have man - y and I don't have much. In fact I
(3.) don't know where and I don't know when. But

*Instrumental till ***

don't have an - y but I've got___ e - nough. 'Cause I
I know we'll__ be lov - ers a - gain. I'll

kow those eyes and I know that touch. I
see you some day be - fore the end. I

don't have man - y and I don't have much.
don't know where and I don't know when.

*Oh, darl - ing my heart's on fire.

Oh, darl - ing my heart's on fire.

Oh, darl - ing my heart's on fire.

To Coda

1° only For

10

D.S. al Coda

You know those love songs break your heart. Heart.

Coda

Oh, darl - ing my heart's on fire.

Oh, darl - ing my heart's on fire.

Oh, darl - ing my heart's on fire.

Oh, darl - ing my heart's on fire.

Oh,__ darl - ing my heart's on fire. For you.

For you,__ oh.__

13

All Of Me

Words & Music by John Legend & Tobias Gad

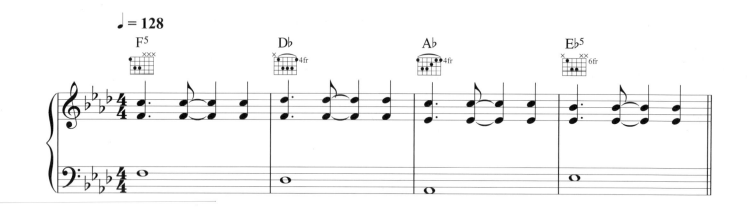

1. What would I do with-out your smart mouth draw-ing me
2. How man-y times do I have to tell you? E - ven when you're

in and you kick-ing me out?___ You got my__ head spin-ning.
cry - ing, you're beau - ti - ful too.___ The world is__ beat - ing__ you

© Copyright 2011 John Legend Publishing/Gad Songs.
BMG Rights Management (US) LLC.
All Rights Reserved. International Copyright Secured.

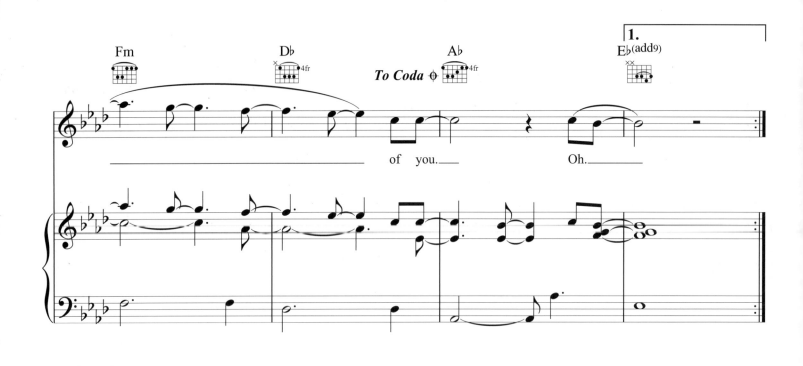

of you.___ Oh.___

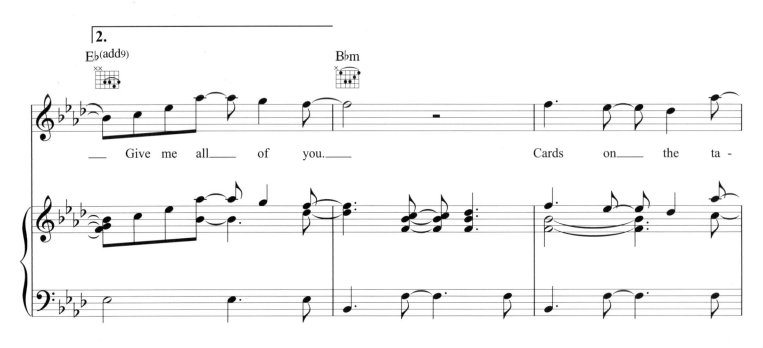

___ Give me all___ of you.___ Cards on___ the ta-

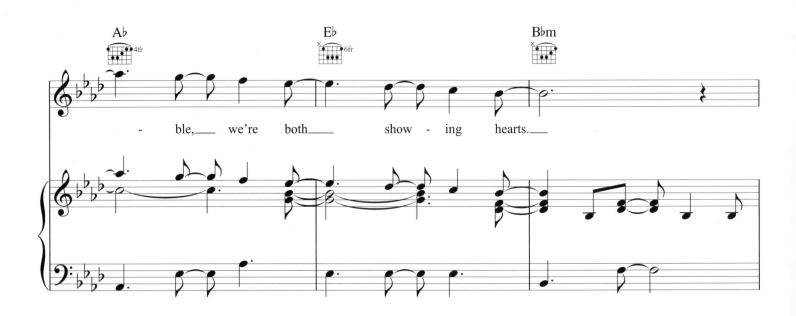

-ble, we're both___ show - ing hearts.___

Risk - ing it all, though it's hard. 'Cause

Coda

I give you all of me.

And you give me all of you.

Oh.

19

Coming Home

Words & Music by Charles Richard Wilson, Andrew White,
Nicholas Baines & James Rix

1. Do you wish you had-n't stayed all night? Do you wish you had-n't
2. And we dance a-long the fin-est line bet-ween the chance of the

© Copyright 2014 Imagem Songs Limited.
All Rights Reserved. International Copyright Secured.

got- ta run. / gon -na come? } Oh may I re - mind___ you?___ May I re - mind_

__ you that you've got__ no - where_ to go?___

So I'm stay-ing be - side___ you___ I'm stay-ing be - side__

22

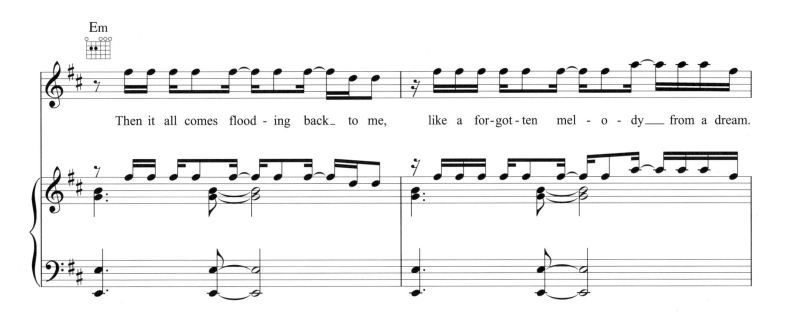

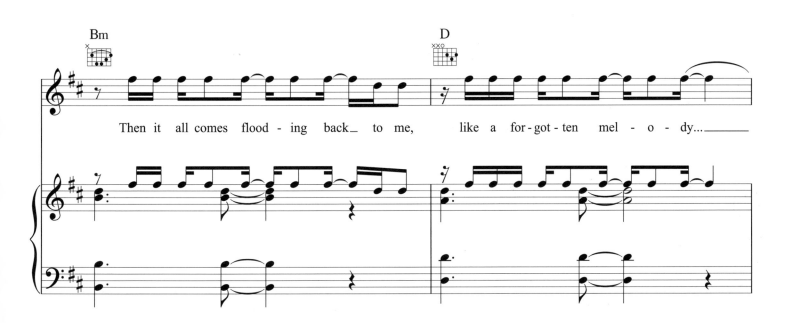

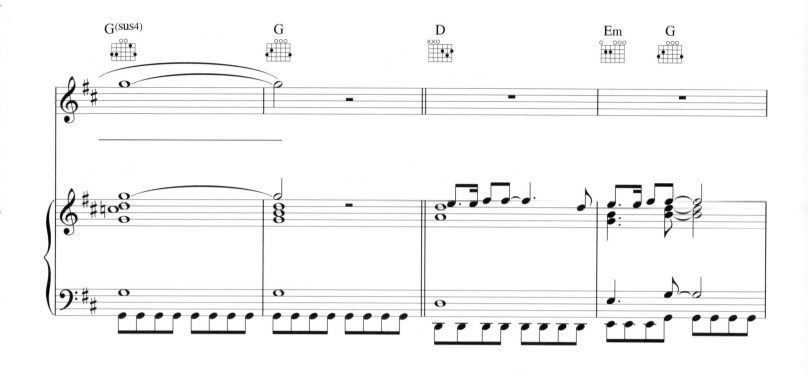

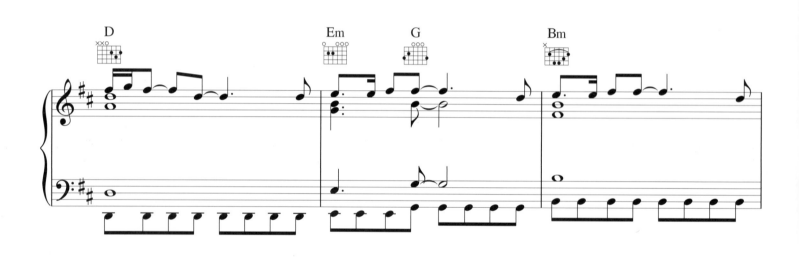

D.S. al Coda

We're

26

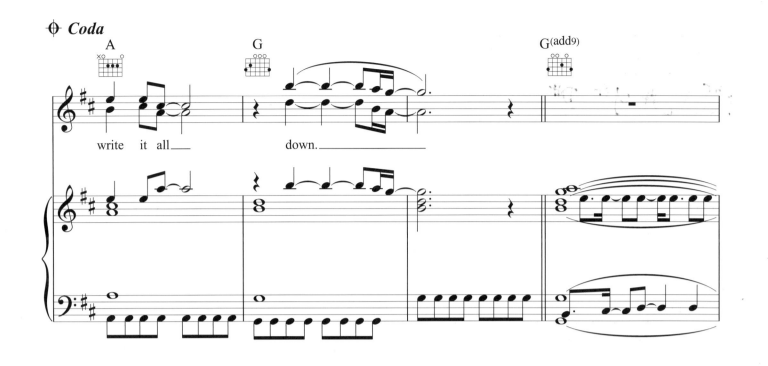

write it all___ down.___

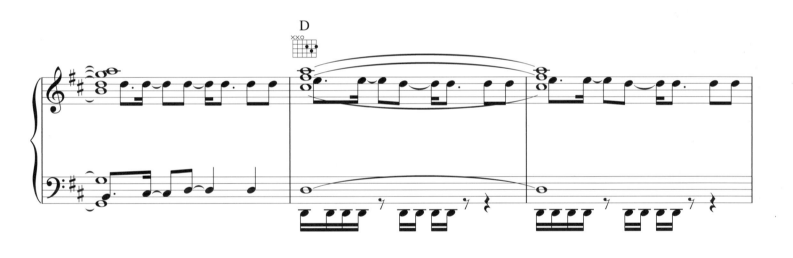

27

Human

Words & Music by Martin Johnson & Christina Perri

© Copyright 2013 EMI April Music Inc/Martin Music Inc.
EMI Music Publishing Ltd/Copyright Control.
All Rights Reserved. International Copyright Secured.

hu - man and I bleed when I____ fall down.__ I'm on - ly

hu - man. And I crash and I____ break down.__ Your words__ in my head,__

____ knives__ in my heart.__ You__ build me up____ and then I____ fall a - part__ 'cause I'm on - ly

To Coda ⊕

hu - man.____

Let It Go

Music & Lyrics by Robert Lopez & Kristen Anderson-Lopez

1. The snow glows white on the moun-tain to-night_ not a foot-print____ to be seen,_ a

© Copyright 2013 Wonderland Music Company Incorporated, USA.
All Rights Reserved. International Copyright Secured.

king-dom of i - so - la - tion, and it looks like I'm the Queen.

The wind is howl-ing like this swirl - ing storm in - side,

could-n't keep it in, heav-en knows I tried.

Don't let them in, don't let them see, be the good girl you al-ways have to be,

Magic

Words & Music by Guy Berryman, Jonathan Buckland,
William Champion & Christopher Martin

© Copyright 2014 Universal Music Publishing MGB Limited.
All Rights Reserved. International Copyright Secured.

And I don't and I don't and I don't and I don't,— no, I don't, it's true. I

don't, no, I don't, no, I don't, no, I don't_ want an-y-bod-y else but you. I

don't, no, I don't, no, I don't, no, I don't,— no, I don't, it's true. I

1.

don't, no, I don't, no, I don't, no, I don't_ want an-y-bod-y else but you.

2.

And if you were to ask me af-ter all that we've been through,

"Still be-lieve in ma - gic?"

Well, yes I do. Oh, yes I do.

3° Instrumental to fade

Repeat to fade

Oh, yes I do.
2° Of course I do!

Oh, yes I do.

Nobody To Love

Words & Music by Cameron James Edwards & Joseph Aluin Lenzie

know you're tired___ of lov-ing, of lov-ing with no-bod-y to love.___ No-

© Copyright 2014 Copyright Control.
All Rights Reserved. International Copyright Secured.

leav-ing this par - ty with no - bod-y to love.__ No - bod-y, no-bod-y._____

Rather Be

Words & Music by James Napier, Grace Chatto
& Jack Patterson

© Copyright 2014 Salli Isaak Songs Limited.
Universal Music Publishing Limited/EMI Music Publishing Limited/Sony/ATV Music Publishing Limited.
All Rights Reserved. International Copyright Secured.

Switch up___ the bat - ter - ies.____

If you gave_ me a chance__ I would take it. It's a shot_ in the dark_

__ but I'll make it. Know with all__ of your heart__ you can't_ shame me.

When I___ am with you__there's no place_ I'd rath - er___ be.__ N, n, no, no,__ no.

D.S. al Coda

Coda

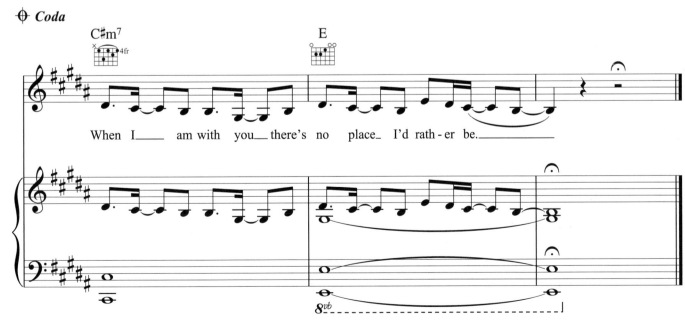

Royals

Words & Music by Joel Little & Ella Yelich O'Connor

© Copyright 2013 Songs Music Publishing, LLC o/b/o Songs Of SMP and EMI Music Publishing Australia Pty Ltd.
All Rights on behalf of EMI Music Publishing Australia Pty Ltd. Administered by Sony/ATV Music Publishing LLC, 8 Music Square West, Nashville, TN 37203
All Rights Reserved. Used by Permission.
Reprinted by Permission of Hal Leonard Corporation.

We're big-ger than we ev-er dreamed, and I'm in love with be-ing queen.

Oh.

Oh.

Oh.

Ooh.

Oh.

Life is great with-out a care. We aren't caught up in your love af-fair.__ And we'll nev-er be

D.S. al Coda

Coda

N.C.

Let me live that fan-ta-sy.

Say Something

Words & Music by Mike Campbell, Chad Vaccarino
& Ian Axel

© Copyright 2011 Songs Of Universal Incorporated/Chad Vaccarino Publishing/Ian Axel Music /Songtrust Blvd.
Universal/MCA Music Limited/ST Music LLC
All rights in Germany administered by Universal/MCA Music Publ. GmbH.
All Rights Reserved. International Copyright Secured.

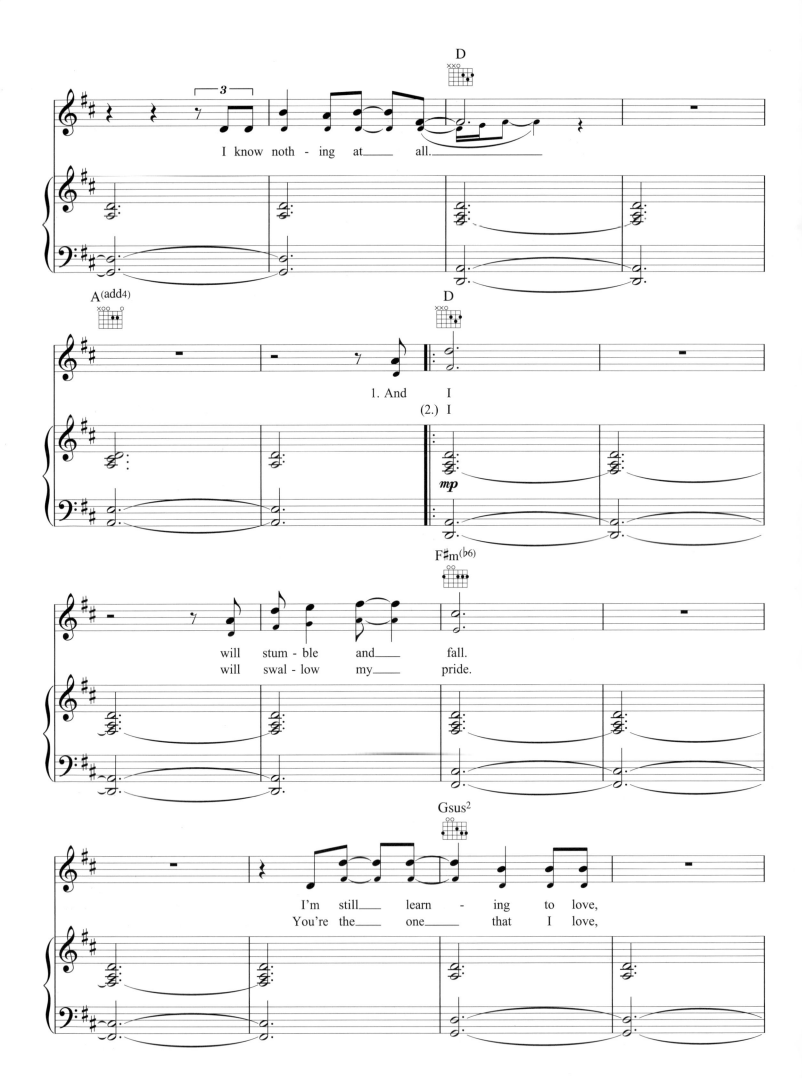

I know noth - ing at____ all.____

1. And   I
(2.)   I

will stum - ble   and____   fall.
will swal - low   my____ pride.

I'm still____ learn - ing   to   love,
You're the____ one____ that   I   love,

Stay With Me

Words & Music by Samuel F. Smith, James Napier & William Phillips

1. Guess it's true I'm not good at a one night stand.
2. Why am I so e - mo - tion - al?

But I still need love 'cause I'm just a man.
No, it's not a good look, gain some self con - trol.

© Copyright 2014 Naughty Words Limited/Salli Isaak Songs Limited/Method Paperwork Ltd.
Universal Music Publishing Limited/Sony/ATV Music Publishing (UK) Limited
All rights in Germany administered by Universal Music Publ. GmbH.
All Rights Reserved. International Copyright Secured.

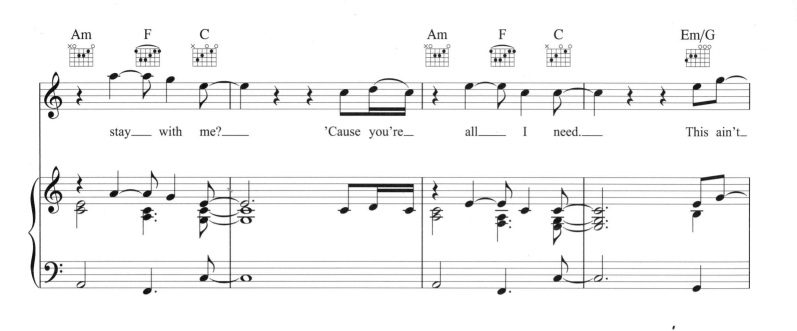

stay___ with me?___ 'Cause you're___ all___ I need.___ This ain't___

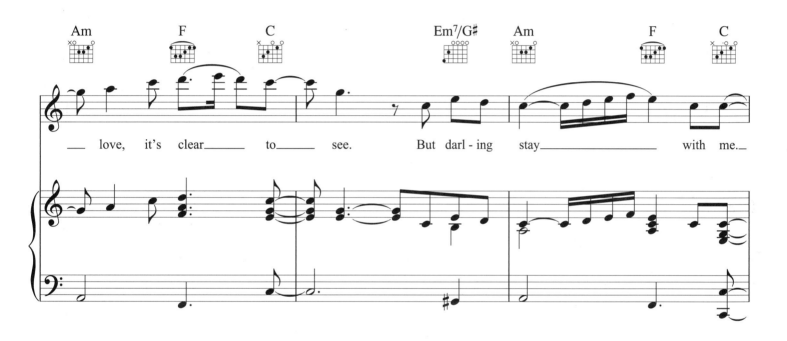

___ love, it's clear___ to___ see. But darl - ing stay_____ with me.___

D.S. al Coda   ⊕ *Coda*

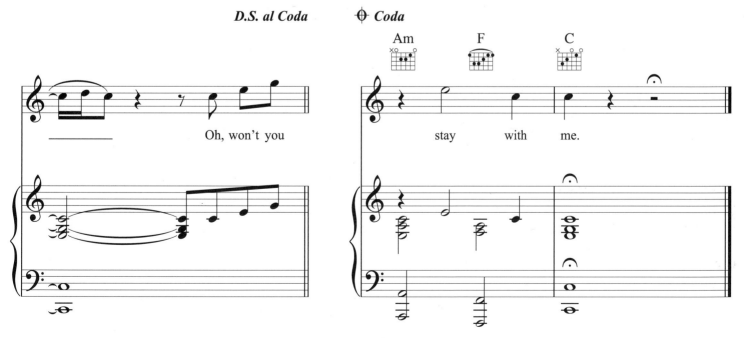

_____ Oh, won't you   stay with me.

Young Blood

Words & Music by Sophie Ellis Bextor & Ed Harcourt

© Copyright 2013 Kid Gloves Music Limited.
Universal Music Publishing Limited/Copyright Control.
All Rights Reserved. International Copyright Secured.

old e - nough.. There'll be a day to take the best of us.__

But till__ then__ we have young__ blood._

2. Some -

77

123456789

Bringing you the words and the music

All the latest music in print... rock & pop plus jazz, blues, country, classical and the best in West End show scores.

- Books to match your favourite CDs.

- Book-and-CD titles with high quality backing tracks for you to play along to. Now you can play guitar or piano with your favourite artist... or simply sing along!

- Audition songbooks with CD backing tracks for both male and female singers for all those with stars in their eyes.

- Can't read music? No problem, you can still play all the hits with our wide range of chord songbooks.

- Check out our range of instrumental tutorial titles, taking you from novice to expert in no time at all!

- Musical show scores include *The Phantom Of The Opera*, *Les Misérables*, *Mamma Mia* and many more hit productions.

- DVD master classes featuring the techniques of top artists.

Visit your local music shop or, in case of difficulty, contact the Marketing Department, Music Sales Limited, Newmarket Road, Bury St Edmunds, Suffolk, IP33 3YB, UK
marketing@musicsales.co.uk